The only Comprehensive Potteries Cook-panion you're ever going to need!

Terry Bossons

Forward

This is for the people who hear the word 'Titanic' and straight away think BEER. They don't picture Kate Winslet floating on a door that could easily fit Leonardo on.

For those guys that know that 'Lobby' is a local stew and not a hotel reception.

If you love the little independent restaurants, you are a great person. You aren't the sort of person who campaigns to get a Nando's but then doesn't ever use it because you're too busy "campaigning" for the return of the Disney Store! Uh?

But most importantly, this is for those amazing people who despise the existence of those Scottish biscuit 'Oatcake' things.

Oh, and no it's not 'Oatcake Day' everyday!

A CIP catalogue record for this book is available from the British Library
ISBN 978-0-9929769-5-8

IT'S A BAP!

What is this?

IT'S A BAP!

Not a bread roll, cob, softie, bun, muffin, stotty, bread cake, bara, scuffler, teacake, barm, oven bottom or batch!!!!

IT'S A BAP!

Now move on...

Titanic Brewery

Founded in 1985, Titanic Brewery has been brewing beer in Burslem, Stoke-on-Trent for over 30 years. Born & bred in Staffordshire, two beer-loving brothers Keith & Dave Bott (with uncompromising expectations when they order a pint) are at the helm of Titanic Brewery. They decided the best way to ensure the beer was good enough was to buy Stoke's brewery and run it themselves.

Even though they've been running the brewery for 30 years now & employ around 150 local people across 8 Titanic pubs and 4 bod café bars, Keith can still be seen regularly mashing in each morning at the brewery (if you're up early enough to see, that is) and Dave is often building bars and painting walls in our existing pubs as well as new ones we add to the portfolio. We now brew over 4 million pints of beer per year with the beer traveling throughout the UK and further!

For us it is really simple: the best things should be available to everyone. A drinker buying a pint deserves it to be the best pint it can be. People work hard for the money they spend with us, so we should work hard to make sure their beer is perfect. If anyone ever returns our beers, we're personally upset because it means we've failed.
We're proud that virtually no one ever does.

Sure, we've got loads of awards for our beers, and we're very proud of them. But the measures of quality that matters most to us is something coming back to the bar and saying, "I'll have another one of those please."

We know the people of Stoke share this passion, because we drink with them every week. And we're pretty sure that beer drinkers everywhere else would agree too.

Wendy Turner Webster's Vegan Lobby

As a little girl growing up in the village of Norton I was always thrilled when my mum announced that 'Lobby' was for tea. I think everyone has a different version of it, especially as it's a dish designed to use up pretty much any vegetables and meat that may be nearing the end of their shelf life. I have been vegan now for 27 years but there's no reason why a delicious Lobby can't still be produced, tasting just as good as I remember it in the old days!

Serves 4

Ingredients:

- 4 Large Potatoes
- 4 Large Carrots
- 1 Large Onion
- 2 Cloves of Garlic
- 8 Closed Cup Mushrooms
- 300g of Frozen Peas
- 2 x Knorr Vegetable Stock Pots
- 1 Squirt of Tomato Ketchup
- Bisto Gravy Granules

- I Pack of Linda McCartney's Meatballs (or the meatless meat of your choice!)

Instructions:

- Follow the cooking instructions for the meatless meat.
- Boil the potatoes and carrots and when they are done throw in the peas.
- Whilst the veg are on the boil slice up the mushrooms and onion and crush the cloves of garlic. Put them all in a pan and fry.
- Add the 2 stock cubes to the boiling veg water. The waterline should be just around the same height of the contents of the pan.
- In a mug, mix several (5/6) teaspoons of Bisto with just enough boiling water to make a smooth paste. Add this to the veg and gently stir in. (Repeat if more thickness required!)
- Add in the contents of the frying pan, the meatless meat and a squirt of tomato ketchup and you're ready to serve!
- Enjoy on its own or with garlic/crusty bread.

Pete Conway's Eggs Benedictus of the World.

Legendary entertainer Pete Conway regularly travels the four corners of the globe putting a show on with his son (you might know him).

How does Pete like his eggs in the morning? He likes his with a kiss (and Benedict style).

So each place he visits he samples their take on the famous dish:

Here are the best!

10 London

9 Melbourne

8 Bolton

7 Austria

6 Russia

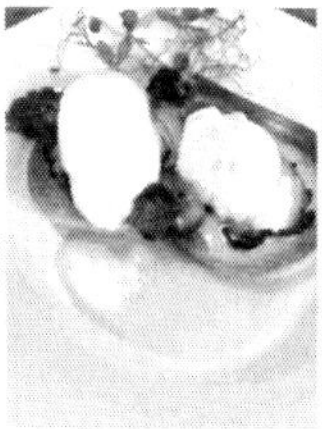
5 Stockton Brook

4 Monaco

3 Heathrow

2 Vegas

1 Frankie & Benny's (Trentham)

Martin Tideswell's Stoke-on-Trent Lobby

Ingredients:

- 550 grams - kilo of stewing or casserole beef
- One large onion
- Four medium-sized carrots
- Third of a small swede
- Two medium-sized parsnips
- Four medium-sized potatoes
- Two beef stock cubes

Instructions:

- Heat a table spoon of oil in a large pan and brown the meat until all the pink has gone.
- Chop all vegetables small.
- Add vegetables to the meat.
- Dissolve beef stock cubes in a pint and a half of boiling water then pour over the meat and vegetables.
- Bring to the boil initially.
- Turn down low and simmer for three hours.

*You can also use a slow cooker. Cook on a low setting and leave for eight hours. Alternatively, you can use a pressure cooker and it will cook within 30-40 minutes.

Important:

"Lobby is always best eaten the day after cooking when the stew has thickened and the meat juices are more flavoursome."

Nick Hancock's Recipe for easy eating Oatcakes (with no washing up)

** Not suitable for vegetarians (because of the pork scratchings on Friday night)

- Friday : Buy your Oatcakes, it is pointless telling anyone where to get their oatcakes from; every family/individual will have a feel for a particular outlet, a feel learnt at the knee of their mother, father, grandparent or, for early starters, gynaecologist.
- NO MORE SHOPPING NEEDED
- Friday night: Go out. Again this is all down to personal choice. For many years for me it was The Beehive in Penkhull. Other favourites for those in possession of a time machine are : The Lyme light, Sammi Belles, Chicos, Maxims, Jollees, The Cock Loft, Sensations, The Comrades Club etc. etc
- Saturday Morning: establish if you are at home and if you can still find the oatcakes. Go to kitchen cupboard and pray you have some tinned tomatoes, whilst in contact with the deity of your choice mention that it would be nice if there was some cheese in the fridge.
- OPTION 1: No cheese, no tomatoes =no breakfast.
- OPTION 2: Put tomatoes in pan, grate all the cheese you can find on to the top and simmer until the cheese is melted and it all looks a bit disgusting.
- Meanwhile take as many oatcakes as you want to eat but leaving one for later and lightly grill them.
- Tip cheese and tomatoes on to oatcakes and eat.
- Once finished take the remaining oatcake and use to wipe excess cheese and tomato off plate; return plate to cupboard.
- Throw pan and cutlery in bin.
- Go back to bed.

Robbie Williams' food and drink top 10

10. Old before I diet

9. Advertising Space Cake

8. Blackpool Rock DJ

7. Extra Strong Mints

6. Pepper Millennium

5. Rudebox of chocolates

4. Party like a Black Russian

3. Pikelet me entertain you

2. Candy :)

1. Angels Delight

Ordering Food Like A Stokie

Have you always wanted to sound more Stokie whilst ordering food in a shop or restaurant?

Proper Stoke bloke, Dave Johnson has compiled a 'cut out and keep' list for you to try next time you go out and about.

- Thray Chayzer Notecakes playze duck. (Three cheese & oatcakes please duck)
- Arl aver mate un tayter pie un chips mar mate. (I'll have a meat and potato pie & chips my mate)
- Giz bains on toost anner cuppa char duck. (Give me beans on toast and a cup of tea duck)
- Ast gorrennyer that smelly chayze? (Have you got any of that smelly cheese?)
- Dust sell Bombay Duck, duck? (Do you sell Bombay Duck, duck?)
- Ard larker pleeter chips playz. (I'd like a plate of chips please)
- A bottler milk un a Sentnul. (A bottle of milk and a Sentinel)
- Tow om sandwidges playze. (Two ham sandwiches please)
- Fishern chips fer tee kite. (Fish & chips to take out)
- Arl aver bafe butty (I'll have a beef sandwich)
- A sosseej n egg sarnie playze. (A sausage and egg sandwich please)
- Chickee Nomlut (Chicken Omelette)
- Tay boon steek (Tee Bone steak)
- Chaze Burglar (Cheeseburger)
- Swate un sour pig (Sweet and sour pork)
- Toe steed chayze (Toasted Cheese)
- A bitter bay troot (A bit of beetroot)
- Jackie tayter (Jacket potato)
- Booler arse crayme (Bowl of ice cream)
- Boyle Degg (Boiled egg)

Shaffers

In 1992 a new restaurant appeared on Piccadilly in Hanley, business partners Mohammed Shafa and David Currie (great name) opened their first of many Shaffers Indian establishments.

Throughout the nineties the restaurant was booming, every week you would see famous people dining alongside locals who loved the amazing dishes on offer.

The walls were adjourned by celebrities and even Robbie Williams popped in now and again and had a Chicken Tikka Massala. Mr Shafa became big friends with Phil Taylor, Pete Conway, Danni Wyatt and even Huggy Bear from Starsky and

Hutch. Jonathan Wilkes ate there whilst in panto with Christian Patterson every year and both say how much they loved it.

They became no strangers to awards and accolades, the bar was awash with certificates. More Shaffers restaurants popped up in Alsager, Stone and Dresden but in the early 2010s a new project opened in Shelton, unfortunately it is no longer there.

If you speak to any bar staff, DJs and doormen who worked whilst the Piccadilly Shaffers was open, they would all say it was the only way to end a Saturday night.

Antony Worrall Thompson's Potteries Pot Roast

SLOW-COOKED PORK STRONG BROWN ALE AND BROWN SUGAR

Serves 4-6

Ingredients:

- Half shoulder of pork
- 2 tablespoons crushed black peppercorns
- 2 teaspoons sea salt
- 3 teaspoons dried oregano
- 1 teaspoon soft thyme leaves
- 7 cloves garlic, peeled
- 175g (6oz) soft dark muscovado sugar

- 3 teaspoons good olive oil
- 50g (2oz) unsalted butter
- 2 onions, peeled and roughly chopped
- 6 sage leaves, finely chopped
- 18 stoned prunes
- 1 x 440ml Stout

Preheat oven to 150°C/Gas Mark 2

- In a food processor blend together the first eight ingredients except the pork until you have a fine paste. If it appears too dry add a little water.
- Remove the rind from the pork and set aside. Rub the pork all over with the paste, cover and refrigerate overnight, turning the pork from time to time.
- In a heavy casserole dish heat the butter until foaming, add the onions and fry them until they take on a little colour.
- Remove the onions and set aside. In the same casserole, add the pork and any marinade and fry on all sides until brown.
- Return the onions to the pan together with the sage, prunes and brown ale, bring to the boil, cover and place in the oven for 3 hours.
- Remove the meat to a serving dish carefully. You may remove the bone if you wish as the meat should fall off the bone. Boil the remaining cooking juices until they have thickened to your liking.
- Pour over the pork and serve immediately with buttered mash and peas.
- Handy hint: a great dish that also works well in a Slow Cooker.

Antony Worrall Thompson

William Carr's Brown Edge Brownie

INGREDIENTS:

- 250g unsalted butter
- 100g plain flour, sieved, plus extra for flouring tin
- 350g dark chocolate
- 3 medium eggs
- 250g dark muscovado sugar
- 1 teaspoon of baking powder
- pinch Maldon / sea salt

METHOD:

- Pre-heat the oven to 170°C. Line a 23cm square cake tin or deep baking tray with baking parchment paper.
- Melt the butter and chocolate together in a saucepan on a low heat.
- Whisk the eggs together and slowly add the sugar. Beat in the chocolate mixture and gently fold in the flour, baking powder and pinch of salt.
- Pour the mixture into the tin. Bake in the oven for 40–45 minutes until the surface is set. It is cooked when a skewer placed in the middle comes out with a little of the mixture sticking to it.
- Remove from the oven and cool in the tin slightly, then place on a wire rack and leave to cool.
- Cut the brownie into squares and keep in a tin or in the fridge.

Dog Friendly Pubs

Dog friendly pubs are becoming increasingly popular, here are a few in Staffordshire that permit pooches:

- Penkhull - The Greyhound Inn
- Stoke-On-Trent - Jolly Potters
- Hartshill - The Greyhound
- Newcastle under Lyme - Capello Lounge
- Newcastle under Lyme - Yates
- Newcastle under Lyme - Black Friar
- Newcastle under Lyme - Gatehouse
- Newcastle under Lyme - Lymestone Vaults
- Newcastle under Lyme - The Seabridge
- Packmoor - Dog and Partridge
- Silverdale - The Crown
- Barlaston - Plume Of Feathers
- Tunstall - The Furlong
- Blythe Bridge - Crossways
- Blythe Bridge - The One Legged Shunted
- Bignall End - Plough Inn
- Bignall End - The Swan
- Keele - The Crewe Arms
- Brown Edge - The Top Pub
- Leek - Hollybush
- Biddulph Moor - The Foxhound

Oatcake Sauce

Spicy Oatcake Sauce was born from the mind of a Stoke/Penkhull born lad. Having tasted an amazing chilli sauce in 2013 Jamie Huddleston set about replicating the sauce when he struggled to get any more. After two years of development the sauce was perfected…although nothing like the one that initially inspired the journey. Being a local lad and loving all thinks Stoke, Jamie wondered how to test the sauce and began adding it to cheesy oatcakes and asking work colleagues to taste it. This gave him an idea and Jamie named the sauce Spicy Oatcake Sauce. Over the next few years oatcake shops around Stoke began to sell the sauce for those who wanted to spice things up a bit. Red and brown are great, but don't knock a bit of spice until you've tried it.

And remember…it's not just for oatcakes!

Oatcake Day!!

Starting back in 2010, Oatcake Day has been a labour of love for me. Bringing the local community together in unison could only really have one symbol - the oatcake.

Created as a way to celebrate the local delicacy, the idea came to life over meal with friends in February of that year.

Following a few after dinner drinks it was with my mates that the idea was first mentioned, and their belief in me to deliver it.

A few of my friends said that if anyone could get the idea off the ground it would be me.

Setting up a Facebook page, I told my mates that if the page got a 1,000 likes then I would get behind it fully and promote it everyday - the target was smashed inside the first 24 hours.

The feedback I received was huge with people offering their support.

A date needed to be set, I picked Sunday August 8th, 2010 as the flagship day to launch the project. The date was chosen as it is made up of six circles and reminded me of half a dozen oatcakes. It was also the day after my mother's birthday so it meant she could have a double celebration.

Taking my promoting duties seriously, a week later, I began using local celebrities holding an 'I Support Oatcake Day' to help raise the awareness and profile.

Being a Port Vale fan, I got some of the players to hold the sign with the likes of Pete Conway and Jonathan Wilkes who were at a match wholeheartedly backing the cause. To keep the peace I also went along to Stoke City the following week. The first person I bumped into at the training ground was Liam Lawrence, who I had to introduce to the Potteries favourite food.

Lots of huge celebrities have supported the event with the likes of Jimmy Carr, Ricky Gervais, Derren Brown, Phil Taylor, Rio Ferdinand and hundreds more on-board! All have been pictured holding the 'I Support Oatcake Day' sign.

Another local lad made good is former Guns 'n' Roses guitarist Slash who I've met on several occasions when the rock legend has returned to his original home land.

I first met his Uncle Ian who came on the radio to talk about Oatcake Day, his memories included Slash catching the bus in Longton as a kid. Ian said he still loves the area.

After that I asked Ian to send Slash an Oatcake Day t-shirt and within a couple of weeks received a photo of the rock genius wearing it.

On our first meeting, Slash couldn't remember if he'd ever had an oatcake, the next time we bumped into each other Slash said he had asked his management to get him some oatcakes, and was disappointed when they gave him the Scottish biscuit oatcake.

As the reputation of Oatcake Day grew, hundreds more celebrities got behind the cause but the most surprising one for me was US rapper Coolio, famous for the worldwide hit "Gangsta's paradise".

With the rapper in town to play a show at Liquid nightclub, I was sent to a secret location to interview him. The meeting went well; we hit it off, so I gave him an Oatcake Day t-shirt.

As I was getting in my car to leave I heard my name being called, it was Coolio running toward me demanding a lift to Tesco. I took him and think he must have tried an oatcake from there.

As a thank you he ended up wearing the t-shirt on stage that very night and 'bigged up' the oatcake too.

It wasn't the only calling from the USA, following the star of TV show Storage Hunters' Jess McClure admitting he loved having the Staffordshire delicacy with his breakfast now.

We became great friends and Jesse told his folks back home about oatcakes and after managing to get a recipe attempted to make his own.

His mother still makes them for people now, and a rumour of the first US oatcake shop in LA has been on the table for a while.

My passion for the oatcake and Potteries is a strong as ever, whether it's backing the campaign to get City of Culture status or putting on events like the increasingly popular Stoke-Con-Trent.

However since it began I have to admit that it is not always been plain sailing promoting the oatcakes special day:

Back in 2012, I was asked to meet a Sentinel photographer who wanted a picture of me holding a dozen, so I hopped in my car and headed to the nearest supermarket.

After three unsuccessful attempts at three stores to buy them I decided to ask the bakery manager at Morrison's why there were none on display. "Are you mad?" he said. "You've got no chance of buying oatcakes on Oatcake Day, we sold out first thing!"

I've learned to be better prepared since - after being a victim of my own success.

Oatcake Day will be celebrated across the Potteries once again on August 8th this year. To contact me with your oatcake stories, follow me on social media: @oatcakeday on Twitter and www.facebook.com/oatcakeday .

The B'Oatcake

The Oatcake Boat has become an iconic place to eat in Staffordshire since it opened on our canals back in 2013. Owner, Kay Mundy had no idea how big it would become and how massive the oatcake is here.

You can catch Kay and the boat at Westport Lake most weekends and by the bet365 stadium on Stoke City match days. She also travels to Great Haywood, Kidsgrove and Middlewich plus can be seen at events that the Canal and River Trust put on. The travelling oatcake boat can also be booked for weddings and other celebrations.

The boat has been on television so many times, camera crews regularly turn up to shoot our delicacy been served up in this unusual, unique way. The Channel 5 show "Celebs go barging' featuring John Prescott and Amanda Barrie would not have been the same without including the Oatcake Boat.

I ♥ THE B'OATCAKE BOAT

Post Pub Grub

After a couple of drinks down the local or a session in the clubs of Hanley, one can get peckish. So I asked Facebook for some Post Pub Grub ideas.

Here is what I got, do any of these take your fancy???

Lee Hannigan:
"Poor Man's Pizza"
Toast with tomato puree, cheese and any sandwich meat.
It's a classic

Chris Howell
The classic fish-finger butty, but using buttered oatcakes instead of bread. Served with a big dollop of ketchup

Paul Rutter
Marmite cheese on toast is nice after a few gins

Mick Johnson
Cheese and bean toastie!

Mike Hawles
Crisp butty

Nick Degg
Grilled Corned beef and cheese on soft white bread.

Pete Piper
Fray Bentos tinned pie

Jordan Brook
Omelette with chicken supa noodle

Lucy Muskett
You can't beat a beef and tomato Pot Noodle butty

A Pot-Noodle Sarnie!
(Photo courtesy of Veronica Anrathi)

Nick King
This can be a bit dangerous after a sesh, but well worth it,
Smoked bacon with fried onions & melted cheddar on thick white bread, with a liberal side splatt of Hammonds Chop sauce for dipping.

Get that frying pon on, you know you want it!

Forgotten Restaurants

We all have our very own favourite Staffordshire eatery, but over the years some have fell to the wayside.

Here are a few that can no longer tame our hunger pangs:

Ria - Hanley
Bonaparte's - Fenton
Shaffers - Hanley
Chancery Grill - Longton
Lazeez - Hanley
Mr Chan's - Hanley
The Plough - Etruria
Tabak- Stoke
Dylan's - Hanley
Jeremiah Johnson's - Stoke
Monzil- Hanley
Capri - Stoke
Taj Mahal - Hanley
Roosevelt's - Hartshill
Reagan's - Hanley
Roman Grill – Trentham
Berni Inn - Newcastle
Fatty Arbuckle's - Festival Park
Larry Lobsters – Festival Park
The Food Court - Potteries Centre
Al Sheikhs (both of them!), Shelton

Taybarn's - Talke 😂😂😂

DON'T TRY THIS AT HOME... !!!

Suzanne Dale from Newcastle under Lyme thought she had seen a great tip for making cheese on toast in a toaster on Facebook. Unfortunately, it all went a little wrong.

"...Saw a tip on FB about turning your toaster on its side for toasted cheese.....thought what a brilliant idea...so gave it a go....... !!.....time for a trip to Argos....!!.... PLEASE SHARE.. !!... there must be other people as daft as me.. !! x"

Entertainment promoter Suzanne, decided to make herself the quick snack on a Wednesday afternoon. She told me: "It seemed like a good idea at the time....I think I'll stick to microwaved cheesy oatcakes in future".

We asked her son, Elvis impersonator, Jason Dale his thoughts:
"My mum's toast is full of burning love, she was all shook up after but got over it. Now every time she cooks we have suspicious minds".

History Of The Oatcake

It is claimed, some say by common consensus, that the oatcake originated as a result of North Staffordshire Regiment soldiers stationed in India acquiring a liking for flat bread known as chapattis and brought the recipe back home with them. What utter nonsense!

First of all, oatcake shops are known to have existed in the Potteries in the 1850s and the recipe goes back much further even than this. In fact the oatcake possibly dates to prehistory when bread was first accidentally baked from a grain-paste.

Bread, of course, comes in many forms and from a wide variety of grains. Wheat, it is believed, is a deliberate cultivation of wild barley; while oats, like rye, is usually considered an inferior crop derived from a weed of domesticated wheat and barley. But we've no need to go back to the age of prehistory and our ancient ancestors to see how the oatcake became popular – for it is nothing more than a simple diet of the poor.

Long before it reached North Staffordshire, Derbyshire shepherds were accustomed to eating portable plain bread, given consistency by added yeast. Naturally the mix required leavening to produce a substantial 'loaf'. Eating on the move, though, gave no time for the loaf to be baked in an oven, and so the mixture was poured onto any convenient stone and heated by fire. Interestingly, when I was young the griddle used in oatcake shops were nearly always referred to a 'stone'.

At some point the mix for the Derbyshire oatcake found its way across the borders into North Staffordshire where, because of clayey earth, grain was of a poorer variety than in Derby. In fact the celebrated geographer and historian, Dr Robert Plot, recorded in 1686 that the wheat in North Staffordshire was 'brown and the oats were of meager properties'.

To make the oatcake go further more water was simply added to the mix, whichserved to make it thinner and more portable. This process continued from the start of the Industrial Revolution when there was a mass influx of farm labourersinto the factories bringing with them their traditional domestic ways. And so the oatcake took hold, because it was cheap to make and it went a long way in a short package – i.e. easily carried in the pocket or the food satchel of the potter.

As soon as workers' terraced accommodation appeared in the towns every street had its own series of corner shops – grocery, greengrocery, ironmongery, haberdashery, the corner pub, the fish and chip shop and the oatcake shop. The essence of all these outlets was cheapness, for the average weekly wage had to be balanced carefullyagainst the rent, clothes, heating and lighting. If anything was cutback it was always food. And this is why the oatcake was popular on Sunday as a staple treat for bacon, eggs and cheese. But mark my words – the oatcake was 'dipped' into the food and was never used as a wrap – that became a trendy development of the 1970s.

From my own experiences I know that the oatcake is a workers' meal. You see I was surprised when I mated out with some middle class children of professional families who had never tasted an oatcake throughout their posh lives. Their houses were located in tree-lined avenues where there were no corner shops. Their shopping was done in middle class stores such as Home and Colonial where food was fashioned to be eaten in dining rooms. Naturally they never walked the terraced streets of the labourers and consequently never had recourse to buy from corner shops let alone the oatcake shop.

And there you have a brief history of the oatcake as I see it. It is as old as the hills and totally unique to North Staffordshire's working classes. It has only been madefashionable in recent times by sillysupermarket shopping promoting the oatcake with ridiculous fillings and a bottle of plonk to hip, but naïve, customers.

Fred Hughes

Crisp Addict

Crisp Addict

Monster Munch and kettle chips
And savoury tomato Space ships
Skips, and Snaps and Bacon fries
Frazzles that dazzle and water the eyes
Chipsticks, Wotsits, Cheesey Puffs
Potato, Corn- Maize, and other stuffs
Taste sensations on your tongue
It feels so right, but it's all so wrong

Crispy crisp and crunchy crunch
Just one bag with your lunch
Squeeze the bags in the shop
To find the one thats full T't top

A BBQ Beef Hula Hoop
Makes an ideal crouton in Oxtail Soup
I need some crisps, I need them now
Flavoured pig, or cheese, or cow
Open the bag breathe it in
Or pop the top on a Pringles tin
Savour the flavour, Do us a favour
Lend s a quid I need a Quaver
Oooohhhh Crisps

I Love You

By Nick Degg

Staffordshire Gin

STAFFORDSHIRE GIN

Staffordshire Gin is run by Jay Davies and Claire Gibbs. They have always had a fine appreciation of alcoholic drinks and their journey has seen them attempt to make a few, but gin was where they actually impressed themselves. Claire introduced Jay to gin in 2016. He had not tasted it since he sneaked a sip as a toddler thinking it was gripe water. They soon became enamoured and began to focus on garnish and presentation.

They both enjoy a variety of drinks and Claire's father had taught her how to make hedgerow wine and she is really good at it but, it's more of a hobby.

Next they attempted cider. They raided Jay's parents' apple trees and got to work with a plank of wood and a car jack trying to juice these apples and at the end of the afternoon ended up with about a pint. Jay tried to make beer but it was a disaster. So neither of these were goers. One day Claire announced that she was going to make gin. They began by creating some pretty nice infusions.

Now they had found their niche, they eventually obtained the relevant licensing and HMRC approvals and procured a still.

Claire and Jay travel extensively around the UK and Europe in their camper van and had seen gin brands from other parts of the country but felt sad that Staffordshire, a traditionally hard working and creative county was not represented.

That was and is still their driver. Not only to see their gin on back bars around the country but to create flavour profiles that were complex and intricate but respected the classic feel of the drink. It has been important to them to create traditional dry gins which appeal to the more distinguished palate. They are Flavours that have to be described rather than named. Of course they have their Original London dry as the flagship gin but Rose Gold and Black Violet each have a very unique character.

The gins they make are as follows:

Original - London Dry style. They distill this through a column still 'Cadman'. (Named after Lord John Cadman as it is situated at his place of birth) with lemon, black pepper, bay leaves, liquorice and cassia. It is creamy smooth.

Black Violet - This is a contemporary floral. It is distilled with black cardamom, cubeb, sloe and violet. It is slightly smokey, peppery with a hint of violet. It has quite a dramatic profile. There is no citrus and it can be served in numerous ways and with various garnishes. It is a gin that you can certainly be creative with. Its colour comes from butterfly pea and hibiscus petals which are infused into spring water form Cannock Chase and used to dilute down to 40% ABV.

Rose Gold originally began life as a Christmas gin and has developed into its current expression. They are really happy with it now but it took over a hundred trials. It has an underlying blend of cassia with a main body of orange with a saffron and rose edge. The tint comes from hibiscus and saffron. Best served with burnt orange and rose petals.

The flavours of their classic 40% gins are built with woody base notes, citrus or berry mids and floral or spicy tops.

They have overcome challenges on an almost daily basis and have learned everything: design, production, bottling, labelling, selling, the industry, the market from scratch. When they initially started production they were making real small batches and labelling and filling by hand, boxing up, selling and delivering themselves. The biggest challenge has been to streamline the production line and to secure a registered trade mark. Both have incurred more expense than had been anticipated but they are pleased that they are now in place.

The funniest moment was probably when they were 'designing' a special cocktail for an event. It took them all evening to perfect it and the next day had forgot which of the many ingredients had pleased them so much and had to start the whole thing again...

The perfect serve for Black Violet is with Franklins Indian tonic and blackberries/hibiscus petals. (the petals can't be supplied)

Jay said:
"It is the everyday small things that give us a lift and keep us going. Seeing our gin behind a bar for the first time was amazing and then seeing it on shelves amongst 'the big boys' was also amazing but it is always the positive feedback that makes it worthwhile. It is the tags and mentions on socials or a stockist calling because they have sold out. Every producer will relate to those but our proudest was probably when we had helped with a charity event and Alan Sugar tweeted a picture of a gin menu which had our gin at the top!"

Staffs Food Puns

This book wouldn't be the same without a few puns.

These aren't just puns, these are Staffordshire Food Puns:

Beef Werrington
Biddulph More-ish
Scone
Flask Edge
The Plaice Nightclub
Keele Lime Pie
Fruit and Knutton
Stoke and Ale pie
Eatruria
Pignall End
Fennelton
A50 p Mixture
Chocolate Orange Tree
Trent Kale
Meir Pork
Heron Foods Cross
Almond Towers
Pie Lane
Hanley Forest Gateau Park
Sanwedgwood
TrentHam
Bunstall

Eaton Mess Park
Hamford
Corn on the Cobridge
Westfork Lake
Sneyd Cream
Golden Syrup Hill
Brown Bread Edge
Lion Barlaston
Eccles Cake Shall
Chestnuterton
Baddeley Green Beans
Silverside Dale
Fig Hayes
Knyparsley
Potter Noodle
Tartshill
Leek Pie
Normacottage Pie
Balti Lee
Knorrton
Aldi Ley Green
Bircheese Head

Staffordshire oatcakes –

May Family recipe
Makes: 6

INGREDIENTS

- 250g oatmeal
- 150g plain flour
- 1 tsp salt
- 14g yeast
- 3 tsp baking powder
- 2 tsp bicarbonate of soda
- Pinch pepper
- Hot water

METHOD

- Mix together the oats, flour and salt, next add 300ml of the hot water and mix until smooth.
- Add the yeast and give it another stir. Gradually, keep stirring in more water until it has a consistency similar to pancakes but a bit lumpier.
- Add the baking powder, bicarbonate of soda and a pinch of pepper, then cover it in a large container and leave to stand for an hour to allow the mix to settle.
- Preheat the oven to 180°C/Gas mark 4.
- Heat a frying pan with a little oil until it's very hot. With a ladle, spoon on the mixture as you would a pancake. Let it cook for about 1 minute, then flip using a fish slice and leave for 1 minute on the other side, or until cooked.

Red or Brown Sauce?

It was bigger than #BREXIT when Oatcake Day posted on social media the question:

"Red or Brown sauce on oatcakes!"

The internet nearly broke as the tweets and comments flew in. Here are the final results:

Brown -57%
Red - 34%
Other 9%

This will always divide opinion.

In the 'other' category, oatcake sauce, fruity sauce, mayo and none were the popular choices.

Sunday Oatcake Shops

Sunday is traditionally the day to get you oatcake fix, so here is FIFTEEN oatcake shops that open at the end of the weekend:

London Road Oatcakes
232 London Rd, Stoke-on-Trent ST4 5RH
Open Sundays from 7am – 1pm

Oatcakes and Milkshakes
1, Contract House, Stafford St, Stone ST15 8QW
Open Sundays from 8am – 4pm

Sneyd Oatcakes
76 Milton Road, ST1 6HD
Open Sundays from 7am – noon

Bucknall Oatcakes
254 Werrington Rd, Stoke-on-Trent ST2 9AW
Open Sundays from 6am – 11.30am

Povey's Oatcakes
33 High Street, Biddulph, ST8 6AW
Open Sundays from 6am – 4:30pm

Goldenhill Oatcakes
807 High St, Goldenhill, ST6 5QH
Open Sundays from 6am – noon

High Lane Oatcakes
597-599 High Ln, Stoke-on-Trent ST6 7EP
Open Sundays from 7am – 12.15pm

Castle Oatcakes
78 London Rd, Newcastle-Under-Lyme ST5 1LZ
Open Sundays from 5am – 12:30pm

Oatcake Annie's
Victoria Road, Fenton, ST4 2HG
Open Sundays from 8.30am – noon

Burslem Oatcakes
9, Waterloo Rd, Burslem, Stoke-On-Trent,Staffordshire, ST6 2EH
Open Sundays from 7.30am – noon

Mellors
7 Cambridge Drive, Newcastle-Under-Lyme, ST5 3DA
Open Sundays from 7am – 1pm

Foley Oatcakes
421, King Street, Longton
Open Sundays from 8am – 12pm

Six Towns Oatcakes
134 Chell Street, Birches Head, ST1 6BD
Open Sundays from 7am – 2pm

The Oatcake Shop
225 Beverley Drive, Bentilee, ST2 0NA
Open Sundays from 6.30am – 11.30am

Dan Dunks

Welcome to the section of this book (not buck) you've been waiting for, no, not the perfect lobby recipe nor even the best oatcake filling, but this, the top 5 biscuits according to me, Dan Townley.

Whilst this list is based solely on one man from Stoke-on-Trent's opinion, it will be taken forward from here on in as the definitive list and I'm sure will get royal blessing should her majesty pick up a copy of this for the palace.

What makes me the person to determine the list!? I hear you ask, well, Terry had blank pages that he needed to fill and he knows I do absolutely nothing but eat biscuits..

Right then, without further ado let's get into it, in ascending order, to create a bit of dramatic tension (Don't even THINK about skipping down to number 1..)

Number 5

Straight in at number 5 is the **Hob Nob**. Because who doesn't love a biscuit that can break your teeth and drink your brew? It's the Chell Heather of the biscuit world.

Number 4

Custard Creams enter the chart at number 4. A staple in any tin and a lovely little biscuity-sandwich which is great for dunking in a cup of tea. I remember as a kid perfecting the art of peeling them apart, nailing the custard filling and then enjoying the biscuit. Lovely stuff and two treats in one, like a Swiss army biscuit.

Number 3

Coming in at number 3 is your friend and mine the trusty **Chocolate Digestive**. A true warrior in the biscuit world but too same old same old and is the perfect candidate to be in the middle of this list. You can count on a chocolate digestive to be there but if there's other biscuits In the vicinity, you know the digestive will be down the pecking order.

Number 2

Viennese Chocolate Fingers. *Plays sexy music* My oh my where do I start with these bad boys, they are something else. They're elegant, fancy, the biscuit is the perfect side of buttery and that chocolate is beautiful. If Hob Nobs are from Chell Heath, these very much live in the posh bit of Trentham. These cheeky little numbers are unlucky not to reach top spot and if you've not tried them, stop reading, and go buy some. Treat yourself.

Number 1

The undisputed king of the biscuit world is, of course, the trusty **Chocolate Bourbon**. I don't think I've heard anyone utter a bad word about the chocolate bourbon as they're absolutely incredible. The perfect amount of chocolate cream sandwiched between two delicious biscuits. They're a lovely chocolately treat when you're dunking them, they go with ANY drink – and that kind of multi-purpose dunkability is what I need in my life.

Honourable mentions have to go to Chocolate Malted Milk, Ginger Biscuits and Pink Wafers (yes, really!)

There's my list and now YOUR list. If you have any issues what so ever with this list you can tweet me, or shout in the street, or send a strongly worded letter to the author.

Oh, and one more thing.

JAFFA CAKES ARE NOT BISCUITS.

Cheats Pie

Cheat's Beef bourguignon pie
By Adam Gratton

This recipe is designed to deliver loads of cosy, yummy, autumnal flavour while taking out some of the time and labour which comes with making a homemade pie.

Pie mix
350g diced steak
100g mushrooms
1 large carrot
1 large red onion
1/2 bottle of red wine
1 Beef stock cube
1 x tsp dried mixed herbs
1 x tsp dried rosemary
1 tsp Worcestershire sauce
2 x cloves of garlic
Salt
Pepper
Flour

For pastry
Milk
Ready rolled puff pastry

Method:

Pie filling

- Coat the Steak lightly in oil then flour, and put to one side. In a pan (no oil) put tsp of dried herbs and 1 x cloves of crushed garlic along with a pinch of salt and pepper and heat gently until you can smell it. Add the meat (using a little more oil if needed to stop burning) and brown for around 1-2 minutes. Then set aside.

Dice carrots, slice onions and quarter mushrooms. Then put all meat and veg into a casserole dish and pour over the half bottle of red wine, adding the stock cube, Worcestershire sauce, remaining garlic and tsp of dried rosemary and season with salt and pepper. Then top up with boiling water but be sure to keep the top of the ingredients above the water line.

Put lid on the dish and put into the oven for 1 hour at 180 degrees.

After an hour take of lid and stir, if you require the sauce thickening add gravy granules or cornflour until at your preferred consistency, then return to the oven for 30-40 min without the lid.

Pastry

30 min before the pie mix is done, take the ready rolled pastry and using the top of a small plate cut out three pie lids and place on a lined baking tray , brushing them on the topside with milk. Cook according to the package instructions (usually 20-25 mins on 180 degrees). Ready when risen and golden brown

The pie lids and mix should be ready at the same time.

Scoop out a generous portion of mix into a small dish or straight onto the plate and place the pie lid directly on top.

Serve with new potatoes, green beans and the rest of the bottle of red wine. A proper autumn warmer.

Serves 3.

Bottlecraft

Bottlecraft has been in Hanley for a few years now and is known for its amazing selection of craft ales and beers.

We asked them for their 'Top 10 Strange Beers'

Wild Beer - Of The Sea 7% - Inspired by lobster bisque. Made with lobster, cockles, seaweed and samphire in the brewing process

Brew By Numbers - 01|27 Beetroot & Fennel Saison 6.2% - A bright pink farmhouse beer, complex spices and earthy undertones but incredibly drinkable

Pang Pang - Bong Water 11% - A rich decadent imperial stout that was infused with Cohiba cigar smoke my turning the fermenter into a giant bong! Tastes like kissing a heavy smoker

Mad Hatter - Tzatziki Sour 4.5% - An outrageously impressive beer. Yoghurt, mint and cucumber combine in a tart sour beer. Bonkers and impressive in equal measure

Siren Craft - Cheeky VIPA 8.5% - A Belgian style strong 'pale' ale. Bright purple and tastes just like Vimto! Dangerously drinkable

Omnipollo - Hilma 6.5% - An IPA brewed with burger buns and fries!? Yep, you read that right. Burger buns and fries. Need I say anymore?!

Tiny Rebel - Pump Up The Jam 5% - An incredible pale ale that was designed, and achieves with startling accuracy, to taste like jam doughnuts. Fruity, sweet and doughy. Yum

Flying Dog - Jalapeno Wit 5.5% - A very interesting brew. Belgian Wit Beers have citrus orange and coriander properties, this one combines jalapeno peppers to the party for a refreshing light beer that kicks with some serious heat!

Wiper & True - Fig & Quince IPA 6.5% - A golden IPA with a sweet jam flavour and fresh herbal notes. Like a fig roll on steroids! Your nan would have loved this beer

Verhaeghe - Duchesse De Bourgogne 6.2% - A traditional Flemish style of red ale. Aged and blended from oak casks this beer tastes like strawberries drizzled with balsamic vinegar. Complex, rich and unlike anything else you'll ever drink

Bottlecraft is situated on Piccadilly in Hanley (next to The Regent). It is open seven days a week from midday.

Jessica's Spanish Stew

(...that's easy to do)

Ingredients:
Chicken breast x 350g
Chorizo x 1 whole packet
Potatoes (as many as you'd like)
Peppers x 2
Red Onion x 1
Carrots x 2-3 depending on size
Tinned chopped tomatoes x 2
Pepper x 1 tsp Salt x 1tsp Parsley x 1tsp Paprika x 1 tsp
Garlic purée x 2 tsp
Chicken stock x 1 pint

Start off by browning off your chopped up chicken breast pieces and slice chorizo in a frying pan or wok. Then add in your cut up veg such as red onion and pepper. After they are cooked/softened you will want to turn the heat down low.

Whilst doing this have your potatoes peeled and cubed in a pan on the boil. Once they are al dente take them off the boil and drain the water away.

You then want to add in your 2 tins of chopped tomatoes into your pan or wok and mix in with the chicken, chorizo and some of the veg. You then will want to add in your boiled potatoes, peeled and sliced carrots and stir all together.

Then add your chicken stock this can either be already made/bought or you can use some chicken stock cubes and boiling water to make your own. Pour this into the pan and stir.

Still making sure your hob is on a low heat you then will need to add your seasoning, I gave a rough guide of 1 tsp of each but you can add as much as you'd like. Leave on the hob for about 30-35 minutes on low till all cooked through. Stirring every 10 minutes or so.

Serve in soup bowls with crusty bread and butter.

This is also great to put in the slow cooker all together raw and kept on low for 6-8 hours or 2-3 hours on high.

Potteries Food and Drink Mastermind

Here is a Potteries Food and Drink Quiz:

What is the best selling pie at Port Vale on match days?
In which public house did Josiah Wedgwood and James Brindley meet to discuss building the Trent and Mersey Canal in 1765?
Which famous Burger chain was part of the old Potteries Centre food court?
What is the name of the BBC Radio Stoke food and drink show that goes out on a Thursday evening?
Which local brewery shares its name with a James Cameron film?
What type of restaurant is Roberto's in Hanley?
Which oatcake shop does The Eddie Hall special?
What is the name of the oldest Indian restaurant in Stoke-on-Trent?
What is the name of the oatcake van in Hanley town centre.
How many Cherry Bakewells are produced daily by Premier Foods in Trent Vale?

Answers

Meat and potato
The Leopard
Burger King
The Takeaway
Titanic
Italian
Castle Oatcakes
The Kismet
Oatie Mostons
250,000

The Stoke Kebab

Ingredients:

2 oatcakes
1 Wright's pie (of your choice)
Red or brown sauce (optional)
Salad (definitely NO SALAD!)

Method:

Cook the Wrights first in a hot oven until it's done to your taste, then warm the oatcakes in the same oven. Place one oatcake on a plate, pop the pie on ttop then add the final oatcake on the pie like lid. Sauce (of your choice) can be added either on top of the pie or on the plate as a dip.

I usually go with a beef pie and brown sauce but may be inclined to try something else if it was for a business lunch or special occasion like a wedding.

Pigs in Oatcake blankets

Add some Stoke-on-Trent to your Christmas dinner!

Add a pig in an oatcake blanket to your festive banquet to fly a flag for the Potteries!

It's almost like they were made for each other!

Maybe leave a couple out for Santa on Christmas Eve?

(Contributed by Dylan Lee)

Average Joe's Lazy Meat Pie

I like to make this pie over three days, because the leftover chicken from the stock you can eat along the way, but two days will do just fine. It's a lazy process meant to be enjoyed, you can cook it bit by bit over the weekend ready for Sunday with some roast veg, and the beauty of it is gravy is included in the recipe. There's no rushing this one and works best when you've got a bottle of red at hand, and some relaxing music on in the kitchen.

The amounts used in this recipe are all approximates apart from the pastry which requires a slightly more definite approach, but you can experiment with the stock and filling – it's part of the pleasure of it.

For all of the Parts:
Salt & Pepper
Vegetable Oil Salted Butter

For the Stock:
Veg of your choice…But I think:
Onions cut in half red if you want a darker stock
Garlic with skin on cut in half
Carrots peeled split lengthways
A leek cut in half split lengthways and cleaned
Mushroom skins if you have them (which you should from the pie filling) A bay leaf or two and any leftover herbs or stalks from.
Peppercorns
A leftover chicken carcass or half a chicken from the butchers of course. And some lamb and veal bones together better but either or will work fine.

For the filling:
A pie size amount of stewing steak (always best to let the butcher know how big your pie tin is /use your common sense, there will be plenty of dough for a decent sized pie whatever your cooking it.)
Ox Kidneys a decent hand full.
Mushrooms - experiment but your classic field are great need about 200g.
A large onion.
Two tablespoons of Miso paste
A big glug of red wine
White wine vinegar

For the Pastry:

125g of lard chopped into little cubes 125g of butter again into little cubes 650g plain flour plus extra for dusting. Big pinch of Salt

4 tablespoons half small cup of water Egg wash

So this is a three day method. But if you want to do it over two, squish the first two days into one.

Method

On the first day.

So today we're making the stock. I like to take a full day just for the stock, as you get half a chicken and some veg to eat after it's made.

So we are going to pop some vegetable oil into a large non-stick frying pan and heat it up to a medium high heat until the oil is nice and hot, at which point we are going to chuck that half a chicken into the pan and thoroughly brown both sides. You should throw a liberal amount of butter in half way through - don't do this at the start so as not to burn the butter but we do want that buttery brown to give an extra depth of flavour to our stock. After this we are going to throw all of our stock ingredients into a large stock pot and cover with water not so much as to drown the flavour but enough to allow for skimming (which is important).

Bring it to a simmer but not a rolling boil as you will boil the surface scum back into the stock. We are then going to leave it to simmer and every now and again remove to scum on the surface of the stock until there is none left, then continue to simmer and taste until you think the bones meat and vegetables have released their goodness and you have a tasty stock.

The next bit can be a bit of a muddle but it is necessary. So we are going to drain our stock. You should then be left with half a chicken some leftover bones and some veg, none of which will go to waste. We are first going to remove the meat from the half chicken keeping the bones aside. You are free to eat the meat and veg as you please. I like to cover the chicken meat and veg in butter and eat with a little bread and a spoon or two of the stock. Save all of the bones from all of the beasts, and put them and the stock in the fridge ready for tomorrow. Day one done your meal, bones and stock up, winner.

On the second day.

Today we are making our filling, our pastry, and continuing to prep that gravy. First step is to dice your onion, then chop your mushrooms in half, they will shrink on cooking and chop your kidneys into small pieces. Have these all at hand before you start to cook as well as you bones and stock from yesterday.

Next dust your stewing steak in flour make sure its covered. You will need to do this until the outside of the chunks of steak are dry, but you don't want clumpy bits of flour so bash the chunks around till they are neatly covered in a light dusting. Sprinkle the dry chunks with salt and pepper and heat up your large frying pan, with generous knob of butter. When the butter begins to turn golden and lightly bubbling throw in the stewing steak browning on all sides. Don't worry about the steak burning the pan slightly - we are after this brown and sticky stuff on the bottom of the pan. Once your meat is brown put to one side and leave to cool. Take your pan off the heat, and when it's cooled down a little we are going to continue to make our gravy by adding a splash of white wine vinegar to the pan and stir and scrape the sticky brown stuff off the bottom of the pan. Once all of it is mixed up with the vinegar we going to put it back on a low heat and add a large dollop of miso paste and mix this in as well. This is going to give us a real savoury liquid.

We now need two pots one for our gravy, one for our filling. Seeing as we have started the gravy let's keep this going. Put our savoury meaty mixture in one of the pots along with our leftover bones and our stock. Leave this simmering away - at this point we are trying to thicken the gravy stock up. We are going to use half in the pie and half to pour over our meal on Sunday.

Whilst our gravy is simmering, in the other pot gently cook our onions in a little oil and salt to stop them burning. Once the onions are soft add in our mushrooms, kidneys and some more butter, and leave on a gentle heat for 10 to 15 minutes. Whilst this is cooking chop up our browned steak into whatever sized chunks of steak you would like in your pie. I like slightly larger than kidneys and mushrooms but it's entirely up to you, then add to the pan with the rest. We are now going to turn up to a medium heat and add a glug of red wine, and cook it a little till you get a lovely waft of vino. Next we are going to drain our bones (get rid of them apart from one which we can use to stick out of our pie at the end - straight lambs bones tend to work best) from our gravy.

At this point we should have a large pot of dark brown gravy that's thickened somewhat but there still should be plenty for both our filling and our jug. Once you're confident all the bones have been removed double check those small chicken bones, then pour half of the mixture over our filling until the meat is covered and leave this pot to thicken stirring and seasoning to taste as you go along, especially towards the end of the cooking process as we are thickening this mixture up until it's sloppy and sturdy to be a pie filling, we don't want to cut into our pie and the middle all run out. The gravy is pretty much done at this point so you can stick it in the fridge ready to heat through tomorrow.

As the filling is simmering away we can make our dough for the pie casing. This is a lot easier than you would think, take your time with it, and combine wet to dry and little by little. We are going to put our flour in a mixing bowl with a big pinch of salt and then slowly add our fats to the flour bit by bit crumbling it through your fingers until all of the fat and flour is combined and you have a bowl full of a fine breadcrumb like mixture. At this point we are going to add our little cup of water bit by bit and with one flour dusted hand stir the water in with as little interaction with the mixture as possible as if your palm is a spoon and you stirring around the outside of the bowl scraping the mixture into a ball. Add the water slowly - the dough should slowly form into a big blob of damp dough. Put some flour on a surface and plop your dough ball onto it and knead until firm, dust with flour as you go so the dough doesn't stick. Once done wrap with cling film and stick in the fridge. At this point our filling should be ready so you can also stick that in the fridge and let the ingredients get to know each other overnight. Day two down.

On the third day.
Todays the day! We have our gravy, pie filling and dough all ready to go. Grab your pie tin and cover in butter so the pie doesn't stick to the bottom. Grab your rolling pin and roll your dough till appropriately thin and shaped for a top and bottom of your pie. We are going to reheat our filling and put our pie bottom into the tin. Once our filling is heated fill your pie, and then cover your pie with its top and crimp edges together. Next were going to push that left over bone through the middle so we have a hole for the hot air to escape through. Next egg wash the top of your pie, and place into a preheated oven at 200/220 degrees c gas mark 6 for 30 to 35 minutes until golden brown. Whilst your pie is cooking you can sort out your accompanying veg and heat up your gravy, adding water or cornflour as preferred to either thin or thicken. And bosh, 5 animals and three days later you've got Average Joes Lazy Meat Pie.

AVERAGE JOE

AS SLICK AS RICK, IF NOT SLICKER

Tony C's Chicken and Chorizo Pie

Serves 4, Prep takes 30mins, takes approx 2hrs to cook

700g x Ready-made shortcrust pastry
1 x Egg yolk, mixed with 1 tbsp x milk for egg wash
Sea salt
Black pepper
1.1/2kg x Chicken fillets, cut into chunks
4-5 x Banana shallots, peeled and thickly sliced
250g x Chorizo, thickly sliced
300ml x Red wine
300ml x Organic chicken stock
75g x Sweet red pepper (either fresh or roasted)
2 tsp x Flour

First brown your chicken in oil and put to one side, in the same pan add the shallots and chorizo, and fry for several minutes until coloured, stirring frequently. Return the chicken chunks to the pan, add the red wine and stock and a little salt, bring to the boil, then cover and simmer for an hour, stirring occasionally.

Preheat your oven to 160C Gas Mark 3. Line a 25cm pie dish with 2/3rd of a block of ready-made short crust pastry, don't trim the pastry back to allow for shrinkage. Then heat your oven to 220C Gas Mark 7.

Take the chicken/chorizo mixture along with the chopped red pepper from the pan, reserving the liquid for later, and transfer to the pie dish. Thinly roll out the remaining third of the pastry for the lid, lay this in place and trim the edges, leaving 1cm for shrinkage. Press the edges together using a fork or crimp them decoratively. Brush the pie top with egg wash. Bake the pie for 40-45mins until nice and golden. Gently heat the reserved gravy and add a teaspoon or two of flour to thicken.

The Coachmakers

The Coachmakers Arms on Lichfield Street, Hanley is a much loved community pub by people from all over the world. So I thought I would feature it as it's a very popular and historic venue in the town centre.

It was threatened by closure in 2010 and a campaign to "Save The Coachmakers" was launched, receiving support from people across the globe on a number of petitions. The authorities however chose not to listen and pushed on with plans to redevelop the whole area, starting by moving the bus station to a new home opposite the Coachmakers. However, somewhat fortunately for the pub, (some might say it was a natural justice) the planned retail centre never managed to sell enough space to make it a viable proposition.

In 2019 the pub was taken over by local couple - Rob Ledgar and Debbie Clarke. They have steered the pub from rocky waters after it actually closed for 3 months in 2018, it's now thriving and has won the prestigious CAMRA award for Pub of the Month for November 2019. Rob and Deb have also overseen the pub having a new roof and external decoration, giving the Coachmakers a new look.

The Coachmakers Arms is said to be between 150 and 170 years old, depending which version of history you believe. It is documented as being there in 1870 but some people say it has been a public house for longer that that.

Other oddities that the pub has include "Dead Man's Corner" which is in the lounge. The story tells of an older gentleman who actually passed away while sitting in the corner of the pub. It is said he would regularly read the paper and nod off. One evening the regulars who were used to his sleep patterns would wake him at last orders. One night last orders came and they found he'd actually passed away. The corner became known as "Dead Man's Corner" and is often the last place to be sat in when the room fills up.

The pub is also said to be haunted and paranormal investigators have documented unexplained activity. It is said that a gentleman named Norman Boyd sits in the piano room with his small dog. The publicans themselves are yet to witness anything or find out any more information about Norman or his dog.

So pop in and keep this iconic venue thriving in a climate that's sees hundreds of pubs closing weekly in the UK.

Cheers!

Wrights Pies

The famous Wrights Pies Company was founded in 1926 by John James Wright and is still family-owned today. In 1926, John started making his pies from the front room of his terraced house in Stoke-on-Trent. The old Wrights Stoke-on-Trent factory is now used for confectionery production. There are branches in all the six towns and many of the surrounding areas. Famously sold all over the place, even at football grounds. The pies are favourites with former WSM Eddie Hall and singer Olly Murs.

What's your favourite?

Fabulous Baker Brothers Bread

Serves 1 large loaf

This classic white bread recipe is the foundation stone for great home-baking and shows how to make bread.

Ingredients
560g strong white flour
10g sea salt
5g dried yeast (or 10g of fresh yeast if you can get it)
300ml tepid water
20ml rapeseed oil

1. Weigh the flour and salt into a big bowl. Add the oil. Measure the water into a jug. With a fork, stir the yeast into the warm water. Empty the jug into the bowl and stir all the ingredients together.
2. Knead the dough for 20 minutes (or 10 minutes in an electric mixer). Once you have a smooth and elastic dough nestle it back into the bowl and cover in cling film with no air gaps. Leave it in a warm place to grow to twice its size or for 1 hour, whichever is first.
3. By hand, shape your dough so it fits evenly into a well-oiled large loaf tin, seal-side down. Dust the top of your loaf with a bit of flour and then cover the tin and leave it in a warm place to double in size or for 1 hour (whichever is first).
4. Preheat the oven to 240°C/gas mark 9. Slash the top of your loaf and place on a baking sheet or a baking stone in the preheated oven. Throw a cupful of water onto the baking sheet for the perfect crust.
5. Check it after 10 minutes and turn the oven down a notch (210°C/gas mark 6½). Take it out after 30 minutes when it's baked and beautifully golden all over. It should sound hollow when tapped underneath.
6. Turn the loaf out and cool it for at least 10 minutes on a wire rack.

Biscuits

I love a top ten!
I love music!
I love biscuits!

So here is the Musical Biscuit Top Ten:

10 Limp Biscuit
9 Bourbon Jovi
8 Dave Fig Grohl
7 Curiosity killed the Kit Kat
6 Garibaldi Barlow
5 Godley and Custard Cream
4 Lionel Rich Tea
3 DigeSteve Miller Band
2 Malted Milky Chance
1 Oreo Speedwagon

Chocolate Music

OK, the biscuit music puns were that much fun to think up that I've compiled a Chocolate Music Top Ten:

10 Everything but the Twirl
9 The Drifters
8 Little Twix
7 Desmond Double Dekker
6 Eminems
5 Emerson Flake and Palmer
4 Fleetwood Caramac
3 PicNic Cave
2 Electric Turkish DeLight Orchestra
1 Thirty Seconds To Mars Bar

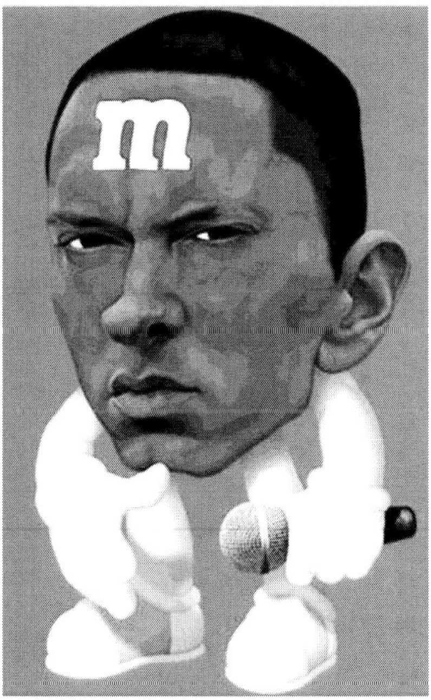

Christian Patterson's Gooey Vegan Brownies

The best thing about these little beauties is that they only take 15 minutes to prep, 25 minutes to cook and 10 minutes to cool...so you can be eating them in 50 minutes! GET IN!

You need...

- 140g Plain flour
- 20g Cocoa powder
- 200g Caster sugar
- 80ml Vegetable oil
- 1 tsp Vanilla extract
- 200g Dark (vegan) chocolate
- 240ml Almond milk

So...
Preheat oven to 160 & line an 8-inch square baking tin with baking paper.

In a large mixing bowl, add the flour, cocoa powder and sugar and gently whisk to mix.

Melt the Dark Chocolate in a glass bowl over a pan of hot water.

Add the oil, vanilla, melted chocolate and almond milk and mix with a wooden spoon until nice & smooth.

Transfer the mixture to prepared pan and bake for 25-30 minutes. Put a skewer into the middle of the brownie and if it comes out clean...it's cooked!

Gently take it out of the pan & allow to cool for 10 minutes or for as long as your willpower holds out!

Then...place the brownies in brown paper & leave them at the Regent Theatre, Stage Door c/o Christian Patterson! Love & luck to you all!

Nathan 'Hitman' Heaney - eat like a champion

Have you ever wondered what foods fuelled champions? Well, I asked Midlands Middleweight Champion Nathan Heaney what goes on his plate to make him a sporting god.

"Hi Terry, I eat the same things most days".

Morning:

I have a homemade smoothie: 50g Spinach, 150g of mixed frozen berries, 15g ground linseed, 10g Brazil nuts, 10g sunflower seeds, 30g whey protein (chocolate or golden syrup flavoured), water and blend the bad boy up.

Lunch:

Microwaved white rice and cold baked beans (doesn't sound great, but it's easy as anything, tastes decent to me and cheap!).

Dinner:

Anything, but still decent e.g. Chicken wrapped in bacon + homemade potato wedges + tender stem broccoli.

Chinese chicken stir fry (Aldi do a decent ready to fry version) + noodles and vegetables.

Homemade beef burgers (Aldi 5% beef mixed with an egg and loads of spicey stuff!), topped with a fried egg and in Aldi brioche buns. Plus on the side sweet potato mash with Frank's sauce and light mayo on top. 😍

Breakfast and lunch are virtually identical everyday (although Sunday I make me and my girls a killer full English breakfast) and it's the evening meals that I try to mix it up. I probably eat too much chocolate and ice-cream at times, but the amount of training I do I can get away with... Just about at least. 😂

Nathan 'Hitman' Heaney

Other supermarkets are available :)

Thank you's

My mum, Gran, Amy Bossons, Connor Bossons, Jaxxon Bossons, Arnie, Shelby, Nana & Grandad Shaw, John Thompson, Jan Thompson, Dave Lee, Dylan Lee, Jarred Cole, Julie Brereton, Dan Townley, Ezra, Kirst, Biff, Tor, Ross Irving, Paul Rutter, Rich Hughes, Fred Hughes, Pete Conway, Rob, Joe Wright, Adrian Tooth, Paine Proffitt, Charlotte Foster, Steven Taylor, Jess Packman, Gary Elsby, Malcolm Draper, Dan Budd, John Acres, Matt Lee, Louise Stones, Suzanne Dale, Jason Dale, Kathy Carter, Jacqui Baxter, The Fabulous Baker Brothers (Henry & Tom Herbert) , Ali Cotton, John Williams, David Learner, Nick Hancock, Chris Parsons, Carol Shanahan, Luke Gessner, The Talbies, Steve Dillon, Chris McCall, Alex Steventon, Bill Hardy, Julia Lee, Tony C, Phil Carr, William Carr, Nathan 'Hitman' Heaney, Eric Kitson, Andy Howle, Dave Pengally, Christian Patterson, Martin Tideswell, Roxanne Simmonds, Rob Ledgar, Wendy Turner Webster, Yasmine Harvey, Peter Piper, Wayne Plant, Craig Longson, Jonny Wilkes, Hanley Museum, Emma Floyd, Damon Simms, Dave Johnson, Sam Baker, Ian 'Diamond' White, Tom Ruston, Nick Turnock, Kev Hall, Niven Ziad, Shaffer, Arnie Marie Jones, Lee Hannigan, Nick King, Jamie Brown, Dave Breese, Rich Lawton, David McKechnie, Noel Sargeant, Adam Gratton, Chris Howell, Mick Johnson, Mike Hawkes, Mitch Birks, Liam Lawrence, Peter Swan, Average Joe, Nick Degg, Jordan Brook, Lucy Muskett, Jamie Huddleston, Alex Povey, Chris Wilson, Kay Monday, Jay & Claire, Antony Worrall Thompson, Music Mania, Chris Wilson and last but not least - Mrs Palmer who was my Home Economics teacher in 1985.

INDEX